An Executive Summary of

Jaron Lanier's

Who Own the Future?

Table of Contents:

i. Introduction/Synopsis

Not so long ago the Internet was seen as the next great economic engine. The optimism was never higher than at the peak of the dot–com boom in the late 1990s, of course; but even after the dot–com bust in the early 2000s, many believed that this was but the growing pains of an emerging industry, and that in the long run the Internet would yet provide the foundation for a new and improved information economy.

Since that time, it is certainly the case that the Internet has spawned a few major successes (such as Google, Amazon, eBay and now Facebook), as well as a host of hopefuls (such as Twitter, Kickstarter, Pinterest and Instagram). However, it cannot be said that the economy has enjoyed a great boost since the Internet exploded. On the contrary, the economy has, at best, stagnated—and it currently shows no signs of escaping its slump. So what went wrong?

According to Silicon Valley luminary Jaron Lanier the problem is not so much with the Internet per se, but with how it has been set up, and how the major Internet companies themselves are organized. To begin with, major Internet companies tend to form monopolies, or near–monopolies, and on a global scale (mainly because Internet networks are able to reach a global audience and undercut local players, but also because these networks are more valuable to their users as they grow larger [for instance, it is most convenient to just join Facebook to connect with friends because this is the platform that most people, for whatever reason, have come to use—it just simplifies things]). The formation of monopolies and near monopolies destroys competition, of course, which compromises economic growth.

Even more important than this, though, is that Internet megaliths employ relatively few people, and have very little overhead (thus they simply don't contribute much back to the economy). You see, the business plan of most successful Internet companies is to offer a particular service for free (such as Internet search efficiency with Google, or social connecting with Facebook, or business connecting with LinkedIn, or an auction platform with eBay, or music and video files on a sharing site etc). The framework of the platform is provided by the company, but the content of the service is provided by the users and/or the general public (indexable websites on Google, Facebook pages on Facebook, LinkedIn profiles on LinkedIn, auction items on eBay, and music and video files on sharing sites etc.). The site attracts users with the prospect of a free and useful service, and the site itself makes revenue through selling advertising space. Oftentimes, the company collects information from its users through its activities on the platform, and uses this information to help target them with ads (among other things) and/or sells this information to third parties so these third parties can use it themselves. (Lanier calls companies that operate in this way Siren Servers—the term applies to any company or organization that uses data streams to garner wealth and power.)

As we can see, then, a big part of the value of these Internet companies comes from their users' content and information—as well as the content of third parties whose material is being shared no end. Now, if these users and content providers were being paid fairly for their contributions (according to how much value they bring to the Internet companies, and other Siren Servers, who use it), we could surely expect a major economic boost as a result. Instead, the users and content providers are paid nothing for their contributions (or at most a fraction of what their contributions represent). The end result of this is that wealth is concentrated at the top—in the hands of the major Internet companies and other Siren Servers—and the economy as a whole suffers (since few jobs are created to allow the wealth to trickle down).

And that's just the beginning. The fact is that more and more things are being digitized as we move forward (for instance, driving is being digitized through driverless cars, education lessons are being digitized through being recorded on digital equipment, and even physical objects are being digitized through 3D printing). As things become digitized they become capable of being shared over the Internet for next to nothing. This will inevitably mean the further erosion of productive jobs (and whole industries—such as has already occurred in the music and video industries).

Ultimately, the only wealth–generating endeavor left will be the Internet platforms that share all of this information—or provide other free services. Of course, with nothing productive left to advertise, their revenues will fall off as well, so even they won't be making any money. For Lanier, this is the fate we can expect unless we change the game we are currently playing.

The long short of it is that we must find a way to pay people adequately for the information and content they contribute to the information economy. Lanier argues this means reorganizing the Internet in such a way that informational transactions are monetized—such that the users of information are charged and the providers are paid for each transaction. It is not going to be easy to reorganize the Internet in this way–not only technically, but also because we have all become accustomed to using the Internet the way it is (and we like getting things for 'free').

Ultimately, though, we will have no choice, for our current course is leading us to an economy that is dominated by wealth at the top—and eventually no wealth for anyone. At some point, this state of affairs must lead to a revolt and/or a complete breakdown.

Here is Jaron Lanier discussing his new book:
https://www.youtube.com/watch?v=j71nj07p_7s

What follows is a full executive summary of *Who Own the Future?* by Jaron Lanier

PART I: THE PROBLEM

Section A: How the Information Economy Works

1. The Story of Technology, Work and Economics

Thc story of technology, work and economics traditionally goes like this: a new technology is invented that allows us to accomplish a particular task more efficiently, so fewer people are needed to perform that task. Many people lose their jobs as a result (and these people often become angry and afraid). Eventually, though, new ways to generate value are found, and those who had originally lost their jobs are able to assume those roles and get new jobs. The economy grows.

Take that most quintessential of tools, the plow, for instance. This tool made farming much more efficient, so fewer farmers were needed to produce the same amount (or even more) food. Many farmers became redundant. However, opportunities arose to specialize in craft making, so the redundant farmers had new opportunities to make money, and did so. The economy grew.

As mentioned above, though, the period during which the new technology is coming into play, and people are losing their old jobs, can be a frightening time. People need to feed their families, after all; and it's often not clear at first whether and how this will be possible. This often generates anger, mainly directed at the new technology, but also at those who made it possible, or are using it.

The most famous example of this involves the Luddites of the 19 th century. In the early 19 th century more advanced looms were invented that threw many textiles workers in England out of work (loc. 2157). The newly layed–off textile workers got angry and revolted. Specifically, they went about the country laying waste to the new machinery and the factories in which they were housed (loc. 2157). The government eventually cracked down, of course, and the movement was largely put to rest (loc. 2157). More importantly, though, is that in the long–term further developments led to more work in the factories, so the disgruntled Luddites lost their motivation for revolt regardless.

This pattern has been repeated time and again throughout history (though not normally as violently) (loc. 2161). And many argue that the same thing is happening now with the new information economy (loc. 2165). That is, we are in the stage where the economy is losing jobs, but new ways of adding value will eventually emerge, and this will result in more jobs and a growing economy.

For Lanier, it is already the case that the Internet has provided new ways of adding value to the system (new value is added every day as people contribute information and content to the Internet and its companies). The problem, though, is that for the most part these contributions are not being rewarded monetarily. What this means is that these sources of value are not finding their way into the formal economy, and thus the economy is flattening out.

Let's now take a closer look at how all of this is unfolding…

2. Siren Servers

a. Consumer–Facing Internet Companies

In order to understand how the information economy works it is best to begin by way of looking at how the Internet's most successful companies operate. For indeed, as Lanier points out, the Internet's major players tend to share a similar business plan (when they do have a business plan), or at least have much in common. As mentioned in the introduction, most successful Internet companies offer some service for free (loc. 253, 307, 2040, 2429, 2734–38, 2750, 2789) (there are some notable exceptions, such as Amazon and Apple, but let us stick with the rule for now).

With Facebook the free service is social connecting, and with Google it is an efficient way to search the web's sites. Other famous examples of free (or nearly free) services on the web include Youtube (owned by Google), Vimeo, Yahoo!, Bing, Wikipedia, Twitter, MySpace, LinkedIn, Blogspot (also owned by Google), WordPress, Tumblr, Instagram, Flickr, Digg, Reddit, Pinterest, StumbleUpon, Kickstarter, Craigslist, eBay, your favorite sharing site here __________, and on and on. (If you take a look at the top 500 most popular websites [http://www.alexa.com/topsites] you will notice that the vast majority do in fact offer free services).

Conveniently for the platform provider, it is the users themselves (or in some cases the general public) who provide the content on the platform. So, again, Facebook pages form the content on Facebook, and 'scrapable' websites form the content on Google's search engine. The platform itself most often earns the bulk of its revenue (when it does earn revenue) through offering ad space on its platform (loc. 3220) (for Facebook this means running ads on your Facebook page, and for Google this means running ads on search pages—but also allowing certain websites to run Google ads which generate profit for both Google and the subsidiary websites [this is one such website—notice the Google ads at the top of the pages and posts]).

Not all successful free and nearly free services on the web earn revenue from advertising. Some of these companies earn revenue on listings or commissions (such as Kickstarter, Craigslist and eBay); but again, for most successful Internet companies the revenue is coming (when it does come) from advertising.

Now, the user–generated content that shows up on these platforms (and which attracts an audience) is not the only thing that is of value to them. What is also of value to them is the traceable activity of its users when they are using the platform (loc. 454, 2039). So, for instance, Facebook (or at least its algorithms) can keep track of what you 'like,' and what comments you make, and who your friends are, and who your friends' friends are etc. Google's algorithms, on the other hand, can keep track of what websites you visit, and how long you stay, and where you hover your mouse while you're there etc. These companies (meaning their algorithms) then use this information in order to help them know just which ads are most likely to be effective with which of their users so they can target them accordingly (loc. 454, 1796, 1803) (actually, Google also scans sites for key words to direct ads that feature related content). Or in some cases these companies will sell their users' information to third parties so they can use it for whatever purposes they want (loc. 1625, 3212) (more on these purposes in a moment).

And what, you might ask, gives these web platforms the right to use our information in this way, and sell it when it is convenient to them? We do. When we sign up for one of these platforms they present us with a user agreement (called an End–User License Agreement or EULA) that details what rights we have (some), and what rights they have (many). Then we sign it without reading it, and off we go (loc. 1288–1325, 2857–67). (The T.V. show Southpark has parodied this whole business to great effect [if somewhat bizarrely] on episode 1 from season 15 called Human CentiPad.)

b. The Behind the Scenes Data–Scrapers

Now, while many of the Internet companies that we are most familiar with offer some free service or other (these are the so–called consumer–facing businesses), other companies forego the free service and just go straight after our data streams. Here is Lanier to explain: "Few people realize the degree to which they are being tracked and spied upon in order that this new form of currency can be created [more information on this topic is available here: http://online.wsj.com/public/page/what-they-know-digital-privacy.html, and in the links provided below]… Even an innocent visit to a legitimate major newspaper site like the *New York Times* invokes a competitive swarm of more than a dozen tracking services, each of which is attempting to become a dominant compiler of spy data about you. One plug–in that attempts to block spying schemes, called Ghostery (http://www.ghostery.com/about), is currently blocking more than a *thousand* such schemes, though no one knows the true number… a common opinion is that Google [http://bits.blogs.nytimes.com/2009/06/02/google-is-top-tracker-of-surfers-in-study/] has historically been at the top of the heap for collecting spy data about you on the open Internet, while Facebook [http://www.nytimes.com/2012/02/05/opinion/sunday/facebook-is-using-you.html] has mastered a way to corral people under an exclusive microscope. That said, other companies you've probably never heard of, like Axciom [http://www.nytimes.com/2012/06/17/technology/acxiom-the-quiet-giant-of-consumer-database-marketing.html?_r=0] and eBureau [http://www.nytimes.com/2012/08/19/business/electronic-scores-rank-consumers-by-potential-value.html?_r=0] are also deeply determined to create dossiers on you" (loc. 1706).

3. The Many Uses of Data Streams

It was mentioned above that the data streams being gathered over the Internet are being used to help Internet companies better target us with ads. However, this data has far more uses over and above just this. For one, sifting through the data (or, rather, having powerful computer algorithms sift through the data) can often reveal interesting correlations that are of great value (loc. 1806). For instance, banks and insurance companies use big data correlations to determine who and under what conditions to offer credit and insurance to consumers (loc. 954–58, 1104, 1924, 2425). From here, the uses of data become much more exotic.

For instance, a financial company might stumble upon a correlation in some data that allows them to make some lucrative trades. This happened a lot during the late 1990s and early 2000s (loc. 1211). As Lanier explains, "the schemes were remarkably similar to Silicon Valley designs. A few of them took as input everything they possibly could scrape from the Internet as well as other, proprietary networks. As in Google's data centers, stupendous correlative algorithms would crunch on the whole 'net's data overnight, looking for correlations. Maybe a sudden increase in comments about mosquito bites would cause an automatic, instant investment in a company that sold lotions. Actually, that's an artificially sensible example. The real examples made no sense to humans. But money was made, and fairly reliably" (loc. 1218). (As it turns out, at least some of these computer–generated schemes turned out to play no small role in the financial crash of 2008 [loc. 1816]—which plays into Lanier's point that treating computers as though they can operate on their own, without our supervision, is both wrongheaded and destructive [loc. 3014]).

In the political realm, data streams can help candidates know how to better target their potential voters. As the author explains, "I remember when I was a young person working for political campaigns, we would inform a campaign about potential voters who might be swayed because we knew our own territory… These days, the central database of a political campaign more often informs local activists of the optimal way to scour the land for votes" (loc. 3157). Elsewhere, the author adds that "politicians target voters using similar algorithms to those that evaluate people for access to credit or insurance" (loc. 1925).

One of the more important (and increasingly prominent) uses of data streams is its role in programming and refining artificial intelligence systems. Most artificial intelligence systems are relatively inert without input generated from human activity (loc. 1586, 1945–49, 2990–94). Take Google Translate, for instance—Google's free language translation service. Google Translate was generated by way of scraping millions of translations off of the Internet and other databases, and then processing these translations through sophisticated algorithms. As Lanier explains, "it's magic that you can upload a phrase in Spanish into the cloud services of companies like Google or Microsoft, and a workable, if imperfect, translation to English is returned. It's as if there's a polyglot artificial intelligence residing up there in the great cloud server farms. But that is not how cloud services work. Instead, a multitude of examples of translations made by real human translators are gathered over the Internet. These are correlated with the example you send for translation. It will almost always turn out that multiple previous translations by real human translators had to contend with similar passages, so a collage of those previous translations will yield a usable result. A giant act of statistics is made practically free because of Moore's Law, but at core the act of translation is based on the real work of people" (loc. 535). And this pattern holds for virtually all other artificial intelligence systems (loc. 1945–49, 2989–94). (For more information on the many uses of data, you may wish to consult my

Though the companies that use data in the ways outlined above are all different from one another, they all share a significant similarity. Namely, they gain a position of information superiority, and then exploit this position to earn wealth and power. Lanier refers to companies that operate this way as Siren Servers: "Siren Servers gather data from the network, often without having to pay for it. The data is analyzed using the most powerful available computers, run by the very best available technical people. The results of the analysis are kept secret, but are used to manipulate the rest of the world to advantage" (loc. 935).

For Lanier, Siren Servers pose a serious threat to the long–term health of any economy. Let's find out why…

Section B: How Siren Servers Destroy Jobs, and the Economy

4. The Monopolistic Tendencies of Siren Servers

To begin with, Siren Servers tend to develop into monopolies, or at least pseudo–monopolies—and often on a global scale. There are a few reasons for this. To begin with, Siren Servers are often able to reach a global audience, and so there are no natural geographic barriers to their catchment (loc 740, 1499). Because Siren Servers are able to reach a global audience—and because they have access to information streams that are coming from absolutely everywhere (loc. 1067)—they are often able to eliminate any advantages of locality that accrue to smaller, local–based players (loc. 740, 1499, 2277–83). (There are some exceptions to this (loc. 1059, 2834), but again, we are dealing with the rule here and not the exceptions.)

Once local players are removed from the equation in any given niche, it becomes a matter of which Siren Server has access to the most or best information that determines which one will emerge as the clear industry leader (loc. 2635, 2823). For whichever company has information superiority has a distinct advantage over the others, and can use this position to accrue yet more information (thus solidifying its advantage) (loc. 2643).

Consumer–facing Internet businesses are a special case here. And this is because these networks tend to be more valuable to their users the bigger they are. This truth has even been encoded as a scientific law. As Lanier explains, "Metcalf's Law is a famous claim that a network becomes as valuable as the square of the number of its nodes. That means value climbs with an insane, ever–increasing pitch as a network grows" (loc. 2636). Consider Facebook, for example. As the author explains, "it attracted people because of the people already on it, a little like the old joke about someone being famous for being famous" (loc. 2630). Apple is another good example: "People use Apple products in part because there are so many apps in its store. Developers are motivated to create lots of apps because there are a lot of people using the Apple store. That's a classic rewarding network effect" (loc. 2649).

Metcalf's Law helps explain why consumer–facing Internet companies tend to form monopolies (or near–monopolies) in their given niche, but there is often another factor at play here. Popular Internet networks not only attract users through their popularity, but they also often organize things in such a way that they penalize their users for leaving the network. That is, there are both positive network effects (which draw users to a network), and negative network effects (which discourage users from leaving the network). And successful Internet companies often exploit both to maximize the size and pull of their networks (loc. 2650–69).

Take Facebook, for example. As Lanier explains, "if a great deal of personal creativity has been added to the site, it's hard to give all that up. Even if you capture every little thing you had uploaded, you can't save it in the context of interactions with other people. You have to lose a part of yourself to leave Facebook once you become an avid user. If you leave, it will become difficult for some people to contact you at all. Would you ever be willing to take the risk to sever a part of your own life's context in order to disengage from a Siren Server that ogles you?" (loc. 2671). The fear of losing the information that one posts up on Facebook (and the context in which it is framed), is one good reason to not leave the network, so this is an example of a negative network effect; but there are many others—and again, most successful Internet companies employ them to help maintain their pseudo–monopolistic positions.

Now, there are many problems with monopolies (lack of consumer choice is one [loc. 2330]), but one of the most significant drawbacks is that the fewer players there are in an industry or economic niche, the fewer employment opportunities there tends to be.

5. The Destruction of Jobs, and the Long–Term Threat to the Economy

This drawback might be obviated if the few major players employed an enormous number of people. But this is decidedly not the case with successful Internet companies (or any other Siren Servers). Rather, major Internet companies tend to hire relatively few employees (even when they grow very large) (loc. 977). As Lanier explains, "the latest wave of high–tech innovation have not created jobs like the old ones did. Iconic new ventures like Facebook employ vastly fewer people than big older companies like, say, General Motors" (loc. 961).

Even then, if major Internet companies (and other Siren Servers) had big overhead, or other costs, they might still contribute greatly to growing an economy. But again, this is not the case. After all, as we have seen, most of the audience–drawing content and valuable information exploited by Siren Servers is user–generated (or user–shared), and of no cost to the company itself.

This set up has already helped shrink the music, video, and other 'creative' industries. As Lanier explains, "the middle classes that have already lost their… economic dignity to Siren Servers are sometimes called the 'creative classes.' They include recording musicians, journalists, and photographers. There were also a significantly larger number of people who supported these types of creators, like studio musicians and editors, who enjoyed 'good jobs' (meaning with security and benefits). Those who have grown up in the networked era might have trouble understanding opportunity lost" (loc. 1456). (With respect to the music industry, Lanier estimates that it has already shrunk to ¼ of its former size, and predicts that once old habits die off it will shrink down to 1/10 th [loc. 1530].)

Why were these jobs lost? Partly because computing reduces the need for human labour, and partly because the content at the heart of these professions became digitized, which means it became easy to copy and share over the Internet. And, of course, whenever something becomes easy to copy and share it loses much of its commercial value. As Lanier explains, "when copying is easy, there is almost no intrinsic scarcity, and therefore market value collapses" (loc. 863).

Of course, at least two groups have benefited from all this computer–generated efficiency and online sharing, and those are the companies that own the software, as well as the sharing sites whereon all the content is shared (loc. 884). As we shall see in a minute, though, the rise of a few software behemoths and online sharing platforms is not the kind of thing that can keep an economy afloat.

Now, if the Internet and the information economy were but a small portion of the economy as whole, all of this may well be relatively inconsequential in terms of macroeconomic health. However, the information sector has already become a major part of the economy; and, what's more, it is certain that it will only grow in relative importance moving forward. This is because whenever some *thing* or some service becomes digitizable, or capable of being mediated through software, it immediately enters the realm of the information economy (which also means it can be shared over the Internet—for next to nothing). And, in case you haven't noticed, *everything* is going digital.

6. *Everything* Is Going Digital

This is no exaggeration. Content, as we have just seen (whether text–based, sound based, or video based), has already gone digital. The next step is for services and even physical objects to go digital, and this process has already begun.

Take services, for starters. Advanced computing and artificial intelligence have already rendered many service jobs obsolete; and as computing and AI continue to advance, ever more service jobs will be lost. Even now, Lanier explains, "robotic pharmacists and 'artificially intelligent' software performing legal research previously done by human lawyers have both already been shown to be cost–effective, and we're still very early in the process" (loc. 2191).

Or take driving. Self–driving cars have already achieved an astounding degree of proficiency, and have even been shown to be safer than humans (loc. 1414–18). They have, in fact, already been legalized in 2 states (Nevada and California). What happens when self–driving cars come to dominate our roads? Far fewer jobs for humans, that's what: "a giant portion of the global middle classes works behind a wheel. Many have entered middle–class life the first time as a taxi driver or a truck driver. It's hard to imagine a world without commercial drivers… And I'm trying to imagine the meeting when someone tries to explain to the Teamsters that nothing like their services will ever be needed again" (loc. 1437).

The following is a very good segment on Google's driverless car from the BBC: https://www.youtube.com/watch?v=J17Qgc4a8xY

Or take health care. Think doctors and nurses can't be digitized? Think again. As Lanier explains, "nanorobots, holographic radiation, or just plain old robots using endoscopes might someday perform heart surgery. These gadgets would perform the economic role that MP3 players and smartphones took on in music delivery. Whatever the details, surgery would then be reconceived as an information service… No one, not even a heart surgeon, should pretend to be indefinitely immune to this pattern" (loc. 325).

Nurses too, can be replaced by robots: "there is talk that robots will become advanced enough in time to take care of the elderly. This is plausible, from a technical point of view. Robots are already able to handle delicate tasks, like surgical subroutines… Would a robot nurse be emotionally acceptable?… In this case… the motivation is so intense that I expect robots in Japanese nursing homes by 2020, and in widespread use by 2025" (loc. 1547).

Or take education. Lectures and other lessons can be recorded just as easily as any other content, of course. And, indeed, this is already happening: free online lessons and Massive Open Online Courses (MOOCs) are sweeping the Internet (famous providers of free online lessons and courses include Coursera [https://www.coursera.org/],

EdX [https://www.edx.org/], Udacity [https://www.udacity.com/], and the Khan Academy [https://www.khanacademy.org/]; popular MOOC hubs include MOOC-List [http://mooc-list.com/] and Open Culture [http://www.openculture.com/]).

The following is a very good segment on MOOCs from the CBC: https://www.youtube.com/watch?v=mSxTw3pXCj4

How long before whole masses of teachers are no longer needed? Here is Lanier on the issue: "The question to ask here is whether online efforts of this kind could create Siren Servers, even nonprofit ones, which end up undermining the finances and security of academics. This is not a comfortable topic. *Of course* I appreciate how beautiful it is to bring great educational materials to people who might not have had access to them before. I have also worked toward that very goal. But that doesn't cancel out a systemic problem that I fear is also accelerated by the same activity. I am certainly not saying there's something wrong with making great lessons and putting them online. I am saying that the overall pattern in which we are doing these beautiful things is not sustainable" (loc. 1494).

Or take manufacturing. Robots are already a major part of many assembly lines, and this trend is only accelerating. As Lanier explains, "one of the strange, tragic aspects of our technological moment is that the most celebrated information gadgets, like our phones and tablets, are made by hand in gigantic factories, most in southern China, and largely by people who work insanely hard in worrisome environments. Looking at the latest advances in robotics and automated manufacturing, it's hard not to wonder when the labors of these hordes of new potential Luddites might become suddenly obsolete" (loc. 1340).

In fact, factories themselves may one day become obsolete. Even now, 3D printers are capable of printing off even very complex objects from digital files (loc. 1360). As the author explains, "a current academic and hobbyist craze is known as '3D printing.' A 3D printer looks a little like a microwave oven. Through the glass door, you can watch roaming robotic nozzles deposit various materials under software control in an incremental way to form a product as if by magic. You download a design from the 'net, as if you were downloading a movie file, send it to your 3D printer, and come back after a while. There, before you, is a physical object, downloaded from afar. There are fledgling experiments with printers that realize physical products including working electronic components. A chip is just a pattern deposited by something like a printing process to begin with. So is a flat display. In theory, it ought to be possible, in the not–so–distant future, to print out a working phone or tablet" (loc. 1361).

Here is a nice segment on 3D printing from 16X9: https://www.youtube.com/watch?v=G0EJmBoLq-g

When anyone with a 3D printer can just print out anything they want (including clothing and pharmaceuticals [loc. 1405, 1588–1671]), why would we need factories anymore? (loc. 1368). To make the 3D printers? Why not print them instead?! (loc. 1396). There would be an industry, of course, to provide the materials (Lanier calls them 'goops') needed by these machines (loc. 1373), but would this industry be able to support an entire economy? Not likely.

7. The New Information Economy

And yet this is where we are heading. A world where virtually everything (including content, labour, services, and *things* themselves) are digitized, and thus mostly labour free, and easily shareable over Internet platforms. As Lanier explains, "eventually most productivity probably will become software–mediated. Software could be the final industrial revolution. It might subsume all the revolutions to come… Maybe digital technology won't advance enough in this century to dominate the economy, but it probably will" (loc. 334). (This may eventually lead to a situation where all of our needs are met with almost no effort on our part—which would eliminate the need for an economy entirely. But this scenario is still a long way off [Lanier himself is not yet convinced it will ever come]; and some satisfactory system, the author argues, must be put in place in the meantime [loc. 3994]).

As the system is currently constructed, Lanier argues, virtually the only players who can win in the information economy (at least in the short term) are the companies who control the software that makes digitization possible, and the platforms whereon the information is shared (meaning the Siren Servers) (loc. 383)—oh, and eventually, the 3D printer 'goop' providers (loc. 1377). However, no economy can be sustained on the backs of a few hundred major companies with a handful of employees and virtually no overhead. As Lanier puts it, "even the most successful players of the game are gradually undermining the core of their own wealth. Capitalism only works if there are enough successful people to be the customers. A market system can only be sustainable when the accounting is thorough enough to reflect where value comes from, which… is another way of saying that an information age middle class must come into being" (loc. 403).

Now, for Lanier, an information age middle class is not an impossibility. Indeed, there are plenty of ways in which hordes of normal, everyday people already contribute to the information economy. These contributions include both the content that is being shared online (or otherwise offered for free), but also, and perhaps more importantly, the data that Siren Servers scrape off the Internet and use to help target us with ads—and also run their various big data schemes and artificial intelligence programs.

The problem is that these contributions are not currently being rewarded monetarily. As the author explains, "the dominant principle of the new economy, the information economy, has lately been to conceal the value of information, of all things. We've decided not to pay most people for performing the new roles that are valuable in relation to the latest technologies. Ordinary people 'share,' while elite network presences generate unprecedented fortunes. Whether these elite new presences are consumer–facing services like Google, or more hidden operations like high–frequency trading firms, is mostly a matter of semantics. In either case the biggest and best–connected computers provide the settings in which information turns into money. Meanwhile, trinkets tossed into the crowd spread illusions and false hopes that the emerging information economy is benefiting the majority of those who provide the information that drives it" (loc. 381).

Because the ordinary 'sharers' (of both content and raw data) are not being paid for their contributions, the middle class is being sucked out of the information economy (loc. 385). For the moment, this is only affecting the middle class. But eventually, as hinted at above, it threatens to bring down the entire system—including the Siren Servers (loc. 480, 2429).

However, all of this could change if the contributions of all those who contribute to the information economy were but monetized. And this is precisely what Lanier proposes.

PART II: THE SOLUTION

8. Lanier's Solution: Monetize Information

Here's the author to explain: "In a world of digital dignity, each individual will be the commercial owner of any data that can be measured from that person's state or behavior… In the event that something a person says or does contributes even minutely to a database that allows, say, a machine language translation algorithm, or a market prediction algorithm, to perform a task, then a nanopayment, proportional *both* to the degree of contribution *and* the resultant value, will be due to the person. These nanopayments will add up, and lead to a new social contract in which people are motivated to contribute to an information economy in even more substantial ways. This is an idea that takes capitalism more seriously than it has been taken before. A market economy should not just be about 'businesses,' but about everyone who contributes value" (loc. 550). Elsewhere, Lanier expands by way of saying that "new data can be created in all sorts of ways. It might be a side effect of what you do to have fun online. For instance, the videos you choose to watch might be announced over a social networking service. In other cases you might deliberately create data, as when you blog or tweet. You might just set up a webcam or some other sensor and feed the Web raw data. Or, your DNA might be measured, or your brain waves. All sorts of information might get onto a network because of your existence" (loc. 235). And again, whenever someone or some company wants access to this data, they would have to pay you for it. What's more, whenever someone or some company earns a profit off the use of your data, you'd be entitled to a tiny commission (more on the specifics of this arrangement below).

Of course, this would mean that the days of 'free' data would be over. But for Lanier, this would be more than made up for by the fact that we would also all be getting paid for the data that we are responsible for (loc. 3772). In the end, information would be not free, but it would at least be affordable (loc. 3269). Lanier calls his system a humanistic information economy (loc. 469, 3045).

9. How a Humanistic Information Economy Would Work: Some Specifics

a. The Two–Way Linking Network

The first thing Lanier's system requires is a way to keep track of who contributes what, and who accesses what, for what purpose (loc. 3524). In other words, the system needs a two–way linking mechanism (to keep track of where information is coming from and to whom it is going)—so we can keep track of who owes what to whom: "if the system remembers where information originally came from, then the people who are the sources of information can be paid for it. That means if a snippet of your video were reused in someone else's video, you would automatically get a micropayment… If someone reuses your video snippet, and that person's work incorporating yours is reused by yet a third party, you still get a micropayment from that third party" [loc. 3513]).

As it is now, most of the Internet is set up for only one–way linking (loc. 3523, 3559–71). Lanier calls his two–way linking system a Nelsonian network (in homage to the man who first came up with the idea: Ted Nelson [loc. 3430–80]). As Lanier explains, "a core technical difference between a Nelsonian network and what we have become familiar with online is that Ted's network links were two–way instead of one–way. In a network with two–way links, each node knows what other nodes are linked to it. That would mean you'd know all the websites that point to yours... It would mean you'd know all the videos that used your music. Two–way linking would preserve context" (loc. 3527).

A two–way linking system requires somewhat more management than a one–way linking system (which partially explains why the Internet was set up as a one–way linking system to begin with [loc. 3531, 3574]), but Lanier insists that it is quite possible (loc. 3531). As the author explains, "two–way links are a bit of a technical hassle. You have to keep them up to date. If someone else stops linking to you, you have to make sure you don't maintain an out–of–date indication that they still are linked. That hassle means there is some initial difficulty in getting a two–way system going as compared to a one–way system. This is part of why HTML spread so fast. But it is one of those cases where getting something easy up front just makes the price worse later on" (loc. 3531). (It is not entirely clear whether a two–way linking network could be set up as a sub–network of the Internet, or whether it would require its own independent network—though it does appear to be the former; for Lanier maintains that some social networking systems on the 'net are already configured in roughly this way [loc. 3505, 3535, 3725–29].)

With a two–way linking system, each person can remain the proprietary holder of any data that originates with them (loc. 3270), and sell this data directly to other people and companies (no, companies would not wither away entirely—more on this in a moment). (For Lanier, his system would also help bring back privacy, and end the 'creepy' spying that many Internet companies engage in—for whenever a company or individual wanted to access your data, they would have to seek your permission, and remunerate you for it [loc. 4792–4807].)

According to Lanier's system, there would be two ways to earn revenue from the data that you contribute to the system: one called 'instant' and the other called 'legacy' (loc. 4120). Instant payments would come from direct sales of given bits of your data (either through accepting a set–price, or negotiating a price, or setting up an auction [loc. 4123]). Legacy payments, on the other hand, would be generated out of a commission on profits earned off of your data (loc. 4127–45) (the rates of which would perhaps be regulated by a central body [loc. 4145–50, 4814–21]—more on this in a moment).

b. The Role of Companies and Corporations

Since individuals would be able to partake more easily in person to person transactions this would cut out the middle man in many informational transactions (that is, the need for the Siren Server would be removed in many cases [loc. 4103, 4117]). But this does not mean that companies and corporations would be wiped out entirely. Indeed, Lanier maintains that corporations would still have a major role to play, as there will always be valuable endeavors that require mass coordination and mass capital. As the author explains, "the future is not predictable enough to know what kinds of big, inherently top–down jobs will need to get done, but it is extremely unlikely that there will be none. Big data requires big data centers, and big companies to build them… Other futuristic candidates for jobs for big companies are stabilization of the climate, repositioning earthquakes, or creating launch structures that make space access inexpensive" (loc. 4028).

c. Centralized Governance

As Lanier notes, the system would have certain operational costs; and therefore, a form of tax would have to be applied in order to cover them. As the author explains, "there will be a cost to calculate all that must transpire in a mature, humanistic digital economy. This cost will not be trivial, but will not introduce an undue burden compared to what Siren Servers already do today… the cost of calculation will be like older forms of the cost of governance, or the cost of civilization. Taxes, whether that is the term used or not, will inevitably be taken as part of the respiratory cycle of an advanced network credit system, as it inhales and exhales money to balance gaps between credit and cash, billions of times a second" (loc. 4362).

Given that the system will require both taxation, and some kind of governance, Lanier suggests that the network would require a centralized governing body. As the author explains, "the only way to create a distribution of clout on a digital network that isn't overly centralized, so that middle classes and a maximally competitive marketplace can exist, is to be honest about the existence of top–down dynamics from the start / We should… be thinking at least partially in a top–down way about making sure that the information that should be monetized is monetized. This might rub a lot of people the wrong way; bottom–up, self–organizing dynamics are so trendy. But while *accounting* can happen locally between individuals, *finance* relies on some rather boring agreements about conventions on a global, top–down basis. If you repudiate that way of thinking, you make it a lot harder to build up the replacements for the failing levees of the middle class" (loc. 5092 / 5103).

10. Getting the System off the Ground

For Lanier, the centralized governance of a humanistic network economy could come from one of two places: either existing political governments, or a massive association of existing Siren Servers who decide, collectively, to change the system. Both of these options may seem completely unlikely at the moment (and especially the latter). But if the middle class continues to be sucked out of the economy as Lanier predicts, it may become an attractive option to one or both. With regards to the latter option, here's Lanier with some thoughts on how it might unfold: "The CEOs will gather at the golf resort and talk about a core financial problem: In the long term the economy will start to shrink if they keep on making it 'efficient' only from the point of view of central servers. At the end of that line there will eventually be too little economy to support even CEOs. How about instead growing the economy? An agreement would be hatched to make log–ins interoperable. That means someone with an Apple Store account will automatically be logged into Amazon, Windows, etc. The same would go for social networks and other varieties of sites. Each site would initiate a plan to make customers into first–class participants who are earning money as well as spending it, and to make the transition as easy as possible. Ordinary people will initially start to earn a little when others are interested by their tweets, blogs, social network updates, videos, and the like. This will not in itself generate enough business to transform the economy, but it will serve a crucial transitional, educational function. People will become used to the idea of looking online for opportunities to earn real wealth… people will start to compete to sell, say, designs to be wrought by 3D printers. They won't think of earning—and earning well—as an affront to 'sharing' but rather as a perfected form of sharing" (loc. 5176).

Lanier does not pretend that his system will be perfect, or solve all the world's problems (loc. 568). Nor does he believe that all of the glitches that his system may encounter have already been sorted out (or are even entirely understood) (loc. 3597–3604, 3829–36). There are issues that will have to be solved as the system is getting underway, and glitches that will have to be ironed out as the system unfolds. Still, the author argues that his system could ultimately be made practicable, and that the benefits would be enormous (loc. 568).

11. Conclusion

The information sector is a major part of the global economy, and only getting larger. It is quite possible that, as digital technology advances, the information sector will eventually be the only sector left. As the information sector grows in relative importance, we must find a way to allow ordinary people to make a living. Fortunately, ordinary people are already contributing value to the information economy. Unfortunately, these contributions are not being rewarded monetarily according to their worth. Should this arrangement continue, wealth will continue to be concentrated in the hands of the few organizations who *do* control information (Lanier's Siren Servers). Eventually, there will be demands to redistribute this wealth (meaning calls for socialism). The alternative is to pay people directly for their contributions to the information economy, and preserve capitalism. Lanier argues we must find a way to the latter option.

*For more great summaries of non-fiction books (including a new one every two weeks) visit http://newbooksinbrief.com/

CPSIA information can be obtained
at www.ICGtesting.com
Printed in the USA
BVOW06s0924310117
474854BV00040B/484/P

9 781499 129564